COOKING
THE
KOREAN
WAY

Lerner Publications Company
A division of Lerner Publishing Group
241 First Avenue North
Minneapolis, MN 55401 U.S.A.

Website address: www.lernerbooks.com

Library of Congress Cataloging-in-Publication Data

Chung, Okwha.
    Cooking the Korean way / by Okwha Chung & Judy Monroe—Rev. & expanded.
       p.   cm. — (Easy menu ethnic cookbooks)
    Includes index.
    Summary: Introduces the cooking and food habits of Korea, including such recipes as bean sprout salad and Korean dumplings, and provides brief information on the geography, history, holidays, and festivals of the country.
    ISBN: 0–8225–4115–7 (lib. bdg. : alk. paper)
    1. Cookery, Korean—Juvenile literature. 2. Korea—Social life and customs—Juvenile literature. [1. Cookery, Korean. 2. Korea—Social life and customs. 3. Cookery, Korean. 4. Korea—Social life and customs.] I. Monroe, Judy. II. Title. III. Series.
TX724.5.K65 C59 2003
641.59519—dc21   2002000611

Manufactured in the United States of America
1 2 3 4 5 6 – JR – 08 07 06 05 04 03

easy menu ethnic cookbooks

COOKING

revised and expanded

THE

to include new low-fat

KOREAN

and vegetarian recipes

WAY

Okwha Chung & Judy Monroe

 Lerner Publications Company • Minneapolis

Contents

Introduction

Korea is a land where the past and the present are often found side by side. Some Koreans live in modern high-rise apartment buildings, while others make their homes in thatched-roof cottages. In the cities, modern skyscrapers shade five-hundred-year-old shrines. Young people honor their elders, and ancient traditions still have an important place in modern Korean society. One of the traditions that has been passed from generation to generation is a varied cuisine that is both healthy and delicious.

Seaweed rice rolls combine rice, vegetables, and chewy seaweed for a light, refreshing treat. They're perfect as an appetizer or a side dish. (Recipe on page 66.)

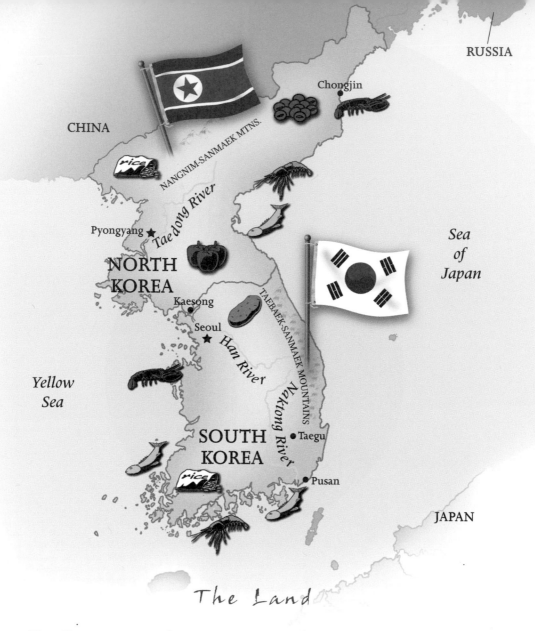

The Land

The Korean Peninsula juts southward from the Asian mainland toward Japan. To the west is the Yellow Sea and to the east is the Sea of Japan. The peninsula shares its northern border with Russia and China. Since the 1940s, the Korean Peninsula has been divided into two countries, the Democratic People's Republic of Korea, or North Korea, and the Republic of Korea, or South Korea.

Although the entire peninsula is only about the size of the state of Utah, its terrain is varied. Rugged, heavily forested mountains cover most of the inland areas. These regions supply North and South Korea with forest products as well as with minerals. Some of the mighty rivers that flow through the mountains are harnessed to supply electricity.

The mountains give way to gentle, rolling hills and plains on the coasts, except in the southeast, where the Taebaek-Sanmaek Mountains are located. Coastal Korea contains the peninsula's best farmland and is the most heavily populated region. The west coast consists of a network of estuaries and tidal flats, which makes it ideal for growing rice, the most important crop in both North and South Korea. As would be expected of a land with so much coastline, fishing is a thriving business, especially off the eastern coast of North Korea and in the maze of islands and small peninsulas that make up the southern and western coasts of South Korea.

History

Korea is an ancient land that dates back to about the third century B.C. In that long-ago time, the area was called Choson, which means Land of the Morning Calm. China, Korea's powerful neighbor to the north, has had a great deal of influence on Korean culture. However, the country has managed to hold on to its independence for most of its two-thousand-year history.

In the A.D. 600s, a southeastern Korean state called Silla took control of the entire peninsula. Silla rule lasted for about two hundred years, most of them peaceful and prosperous. By the 900s, however, the government had become very weak and several groups fought for control of the country.

After years of confusion, a general named Wang Kon took over the government of the country and the peninsula was peaceful once again. Wang Kon is probably best remembered for renaming the country Koryo, the source of the word Korea. Education and the arts were important to Wang Kon and the Koryo kings that followed him. But this peaceful period was not to last. In the 1200s, Mongol warriors from the north took over the country and controlled it for about one hundred years. After the Mongols were defeated, another general, Yi Songgye, became Koryo's new ruler.

Yi and his descendants ruled the country, which Yi called Choson, from 1392 until 1910. During the Yi dynasty, the peninsula was plagued with frequent invasions by the Chinese and Japanese. By the 1600s, the people of Choson were so tired of fighting off their neighbors that they closed the country to foreigners. For two hundred years, Koreans lived in isolation from the rest of the world. At that time, their country was known as the Hermit Kingdom.

The 1900s were a troubled century for Korea. After forcing the Hermit Kingdom to open its ports to other countries in 1876, Japan completely took over the country in 1910. The harsh rule of the Japanese lasted until 1945 when Japan was defeated in World War II (1939–1945).

Rather than regaining its freedom after the war, however, the Korean Peninsula was occupied by the former Soviet Union in the north and by the United States in the south. Because no one was able to agree on who should rule the country, it was split into two separate countries. North Korea was controlled by Communists and South Korea was strongly anti-Communist.

Both North and South Korea wanted to rule the entire peninsula, not just one half. In 1950 North Korea invaded South Korea. The war that followed lasted three years, but resolved very little. In modern times, the Korean Peninsula is still two separate countries with two very different forms of government.

The Food

Political differences have not prevented the people of North and South Korea from continuing to share a cuisine. Just as Koreans on both sides of the border have a common history, you will find the same kinds of foods and cooking methods in Pyongyang in the north as you will in the southern city of Seoul.

When you sit down to your first Korean meal, you will probably immediately notice the similarities to other Asian cuisines. Like the Chinese and the Japanese, the Koreans eat with chopsticks, which means that the food is usually cut into bite-sized pieces that are easy

Korean cooks use an abundance of fresh produce, so markets such as this one in Seoul are frequently crowded with shoppers stocking up for the day's meals.

A typical Korean meal will have many and varied dishes, all of which are sampled.
This South Korean woman is preparing the evening meal for her family.

to pick up. Many of the ingredients—such as cellophane noodles, soy sauce, tofu, and a variety of fresh vegetables—as well as some of the cooking methods, including stir-frying, steaming, and braising, are used in other countries in the Far East. But there are also elements of Korean cuisine that make it deliciously different.

The way that Koreans eat their meals has been called "grazing." At the table, family and friends pick and choose from among the many foods set out in little dishes.

With white rice as the basic food, diners may add something fiery—usually kimchi, the famous pickled vegetable. Next they might pick a food that is spicy with sesame oil, pepper, soy sauce, and garlic. The wide choice of vegetables, salads, and pickles is called *panchan*. It is limited only by the cook's skill at mixing and matching basic foods.

Korean food is often highly seasoned, usually with a combination of garlic, ginger, red or black pepper, green onions, soy sauce, sesame seeds, and sesame oil. These dishes are served with a bland grain to cool the heat of the spices. Rice is present at every meal, but you may also find barley, buckwheat, millet, or wheat.

Koreans eat less meat than people in other parts of the world. Red meat is expensive in both North and South Korea, so it is usually reserved for special occasions. Chicken and fish are more plentiful.

Korean cuisine offers a vast assortment of vegetarian dishes. Protein-rich soybean products are often eaten instead of meat. The soybean is the main ingredient in tofu, a common meat substitute. This versatile plant is also used to make soybean pastes and sauces, including the slightly sweet Korean soy sauce, which are used in soups and other dishes. Unlike other Asian cuisines, Korean cuisine includes many uncooked vegetables, frequently served in the form of salads and pickles.

The cuisine of Korea does not vary widely from region to region. Koreans do try, however, to make use of the fruits and vegetables that are in season, and they try to serve heartier fare during the colder months.

Holidays and Festivals

In South Korea, good food is always an important part of any holiday or festival. Two important holidays are Ch'u-sok in the fall and Sol in late winter.

Ch'u-sok, the Harvest Moon Festival, is celebrated on the fifteenth day of the eighth month of the lunar year, sometime during September or early October. It has been called the Korean Thanksgiving Day. This is the time of the harvesting of fruits and grains. It is also a time to view the full moon. First the family visits the graves of its ancestors, honoring them with deep bows and an altar laden with food. Friends and family share a wonderful meal of taro (a starchy root vegetable) soup, zucchini pancakes, fruits and vegetables of the season, and rice cakes. These cakes are shaped like crescent moons and filled with bean paste or sesame seeds mixed with honey.

Sol, the lunar new year, comes sometime between late January and late February. Because Koreans also have a two-day New Year holiday January 1 and 2, Sol has been called Folklore Day since 1985. Both Sol and January 1 and 2 are times to greet the new year and to show respect for elders. Family members bow before photographs of previous generations. At these holidays, tables are crowded with many kinds of sweet and savory cakes, beef-rice cake soup, egg rolls, meat dumplings, fried fish, broiled beef, kimchi, sweetened rice, candied lotus root and ginger, date balls, chestnut balls, and fresh fruit. The beef-rice cake soup, called *ttok-kuk*, is also served to friends, neighbors, and business associates paying calls at the home to show respect.

The first full moon of the lunar year, fifteen days after Sol, is a festival called Tae-bo-rum, an ancient day of worship. Very devout families keep torches burning all night long. Some people set off firecrackers and crack nuts to scare off evil spirits. Children and grown-ups alike keep watch for the rising of the moon. Seeing the moon rise is believed to bring good luck for the whole year. Farmers believe the color of the moon reveals the weather to come. A pale moon means too much rain and a red moon means too little rain, while a golden moon means excellent weather. Every year, Koreans eat a special dish of rice, barley, millet, and red and black beans at this festival. Besides this five-grain dish, they also eat vegetables and various nuts, especially chestnuts, pine nuts, and walnuts.

Although South Korea has many religions, a large number of inhabitants are Buddhists. Buddhism is based on the teachings of

Traditionally dressed South Korean girls dance with fans on a street in Seoul to celebrate Buddha's birthday.

Buddha, the Indian sage-philosopher who lived 2,500 years ago. His birthday has been a national holiday in South Korea since 1975. It falls on the eighth day of the fourth lunar month, usually sometime in May.

Buddhism has inspired many beautiful temples, pagodas, and statues. During the holiday, Buddhists put on their best clothes and go to the temple to pray. In the evening, after a festive meal, they parade through the streets with lanterns. The light of the lanterns is meant to ward off human hardship and hopelessness.

The children of South Korea are treated to their favorite foods on Children's Day, May 5. This national holiday celebrates both girls and boys. It replaces Boy's Day, which had been observed since the peninsula was a Japanese colony (1910–1945). Parades, pageants, and presentations of martial arts are held on this child-centered holiday. Families, including grandparents, enjoy outings to zoos, movies, or parks.

A beloved longtime folk festival is Tan-o Day or Swing Day. It comes on the fifth day of the fifth lunar month, when spring is at its peak. Girls learn to swing standing up when they are small, and continue to swing this way as adults. Swing Day brings contests with girls and women swinging back and forth wearing their colorful traditional costumes. As they do on most special days during warm weather, Koreans pack a bountiful picnic, including seaweed rice rolls, to enjoy outdoors.

Young girls, noted for their thick black hair, look forward to Shampoo Day, or Yadu Nal, which takes place on June 15. If at all possible, families visit friends whose home is next to a stream or a waterfall. The highlight of the day is bathing, hair and all, in the clear water to ward off fevers for the rest of the year. A typical picnic meal includes dumplings, sweet cakes, grilled fish, and watermelon.

Many celebrations in Korean culture are accompanied by a delightful meal. Koreans look forward to these holidays and festivals because they love to celebrate with the tantalizing, fragrant foods that are served.

How to Eat with Chopsticks

Chopsticks are not difficult to manage once you have learned the basic technique. The key to using them is to hold the inside stick still while moving the outside stick back and forth. The pair then acts as pincers to pick up pieces of food.

Hold the thicker end of the first chopstick in the crook of your thumb, resting the lower part lightly against the inside of your ring finger. Then put the second chopstick between the tips of your index and middle fingers and hold it with your thumb, much as you would hold a pencil. Now you can make the outer chopstick move by bending your index and middle fingers toward the inside chopstick. The tips of the two sticks should come together like pincers when you bend your fingers. Once you get a feel for the technique, just keep practicing. Soon you'll be an expert!

Koreans and people in many other cultures around the world use chopsticks. In this photo, a girl in China uses her chopsticks to eat a plate of rice.

Before You Begin

Korean cooking makes use of some ingredients that you may not know. Sometimes special cookware is used, too, although the recipes in this book can easily be prepared with ordinary utensils and pans.

The most important thing you need to know before you start is how to be a careful cook. On the following page, you'll find a few rules that will make your cooking experience safe, fun, and easy. Next, take a look at the "dictionary" of utensils, terms, and special ingredients. You may also want to read the list of tips on preparing healthy, low-fat meals.

When you've picked out a recipe to try, read through it from beginning to end. Now you are ready to shop for ingredients and to organize the cookware you will need. Once you have assembled everything, you're ready to begin cooking. Keep in mind that one special feature of Korean cuisine is stir-frying. This cooking technique is very efficient, but it's important to prepare all of your ingredients before you actually start stir-frying. Measure out the spices and herbs, wash any fresh vegetables, and do all of the cutting and chopping called for in the recipe *before* you heat up the oil. Then, once the oil is hot, you'll be able to add each ingredient quickly and easily.

Korean dumplings, or mandu, *are a favorite among children. Families make large batches for celebrations. (Recipe on page 56.)*

The Careful Cook

Whenever you cook, there are certain safety rules you must always keep in mind. Even experienced cooks follow these rules when they are in the kitchen.

- Always wash your hands before handling food. Thoroughly wash all raw vegetables and fruits to remove dirt, chemicals, and insecticides. Wash uncooked poultry, fish, and meat under cold water.
- Use a cutting board when cutting up vegetables and fruits. Don't cut them up in your hand! And be sure to cut in a direction *away* from you and your fingers.
- Long hair or loose clothing can easily catch fire if brought near the burners of a stove. If you have long hair, tie it back before you start cooking.
- Turn all pot handles toward the back of the stove so that you will not catch your sleeves or jewelry on them. This is especially important when younger brothers and sisters are around. They could easily knock off a pot and get burned.
- Always use a pot holder to steady hot pots or to take pans out of the oven. Don't use a wet cloth on a hot pan because the steam it produces could burn you.
- Lift the lid of a steaming pot with the opening away from you so that you will not get burned.
- If you get burned, hold the burn under cold running water. Do not put grease or butter on it. Cold water helps to take the heat out, but grease or butter will only keep it in.
- If grease or cooking oil catches fire, throw baking soda or salt at the bottom of the flame to put it out. (Water will *not* put out a grease fire.) Call for help, and try to turn all the stove burners to "off."

Cooking Utensils

charcoal grill—A type of stove in which charcoal provides the heat and food is placed on a metal grate above the coals

colander—A bowl-shaped dish with holes in it that is used for washing or draining food

pastry brush—A small brush with nylon bristles used for coating food with melted butter or other liquids

skewer—A thin wooden or metal stick used to hold small pieces of meat or vegetables for broiling or grilling

steamer—A utensil designed for cooking food with steam. Asian steamers have tight-fitting lids and racks for holding the food.

wok—A pot with a rounded bottom and sloping sides, ideally suited for stir-frying foods. A large frying pan will work as a substitute.

Cooking Terms

beat—To stir rapidly in a circular motion

boil—To heat a liquid over high heat until bubbles form and rise rapidly to the surface

broil—To cook directly under a heat source so that the side of the food facing the heat cooks rapidly

chill—To refrigerate a food until it is the desired temperature

fluff—To gently separate small pieces of food, such as grains of rice, that have gotten clumped together

garnish—To decorate with a small piece of food

grill—To cook over hot charcoal

marinate—To soak food in a liquid to add flavor and to tenderize it

shred—To tear or cut into small pieces, either by hand or with a grater simmer—To cook in liquid kept just below its boiling point

steam—To cook food with the steam from boiling water

stir-fry—To quickly cook bite-sized pieces of food in a small amount of oil over high heat

toss—To lightly mix pieces of food together

Special Ingredients

barley—A small, oval grain used in soups, stews, and side dishes

bean sprouts—Sprouts from the mung bean. For best flavor and texture, use fresh sprouts.

black mushrooms—Dried, fragrant mushrooms available at Asian groceries. Black mushrooms may also be labeled black fungi.

cayenne pepper—Hot pungent powder made from dried tropical chili peppers. Cayenne may also be labeled red pepper.

cellophane noodles—Fine, clear, thin noodles made from mung beans. Cellophane noodles are also called mung bean threads, transparent noodles, or sai fun. They are sold in bundles.

Chinese cabbage—A pale green vegetable with broad, tightly packed leaves. It may also be called celery cabbage or napa cabbage.

cod—A freshwater fish with lean, firm flesh

crushed red pepper flakes—Dried pieces of hot red peppers used to give a spicy flavor to food

daikon radish—A large Asian radish with sweet or sharp flavor

ginger root—A knobby, light brown root which is grated or sliced to add a peppery, slightly sweet flavor to foods. To prepare fresh ginger root, peel skin off a section and use a grater to grate the amount called for. Do not substitute dried ground ginger in a recipe calling for fresh ginger, as the taste is quite different.

haddock—A low-fat saltwater fish with mild flavor and firm texture

millet—A tiny, round, golden grain that is a staple in the diet of one-third of the world's population. It is cooked with water like rice. Millet is sold at health food stores and food co-ops.

oyster sauce—A thick, dark brown sauce made from oysters, brine, and soy sauce. It adds a richness to foods without changing their flavor.

pine nuts—Nuts that grow inside pine cones. Keep them in the refrigerator and use within three months. Also called pignolia nuts.

rice cakes—Cooked sticky rice that has been pounded and formed into rounds. Frozen precooked rice cakes are sold in Asian markets.

rice vinegar—A mild vinegar made from fermented rice

romaine lettuce—A lettuce with long, crisp, upright leaves

seaweed or sea vegetable—Kombu, laver, and nori are the names that various types of seaweed are sold under. Seaweed has been harvested from the sea by Asian cultures for centuries. Sheets of the blackish green nori are widely available thanks to the popularity of sushi.

sesame oil—The reddish brown oil pressed from toasted sesame seeds. It is used for seasoning, not frying.

sesame seeds—Tiny beige seeds with a nutty, somewhat sweet flavor

sole—Lemon sole and other types of sole sold in the United States are actually members of the flounder family. They are popular and versatile fish.

soy sauce—A dark brown, salty sauce made from soybeans and other ingredients that is used to flavor Asian foods

tofu—A processed curd made from soybeans. Tofu is an important protein source in Asia. It may be labeled soybean curd or bean curd, and sold in blocks labeled soft, silken, or firm.

whitefish—A member of the salmon family. It is named for its firm, white flesh. This fish is high in fat and mild in flavor.

wonton skins—Small, thin squares or rounds of soft dough made from flour, water, and eggs

Healthy and Low-Fat Cooking Tips

Many modern cooks are concerned about preparing healthy, low-fat meals. Fortunately, there are simple ways to reduce the fat content of most dishes. Here are a few tips for adapting the recipes in this book. Throughout the book, you'll also find specific suggestions for individual recipes—and don't worry, they'll still taste delicious.

When adapting recipes, it's best to prepare a recipe just the way it's printed the first time to get an idea of the flavor and texture. Then the next time you make the recipe, try substituting.

For recipes calling for beef or pork, use a sharp knife to cut off excess fat. For recipes using chicken, use kitchen shears to trim excess fat under edges of chicken skin on breasts and thighs before cooking. Since chicken skin is fatty, cook the food with skin on for flavor, then remove skin before serving.

Try using a vegetable oil spray on the skillet, rather than oil, before browning or frying foods. These sprays are available in low-fat and nonfat varieties

When a dish combines meat and vegetables, experiment with cutting the amount of meat in half and doubling the amount of vegetables. Another way to reduce fat in combination dishes is to use cut-up tofu in place of some or all of the meat, adding the tofu at the same time as the vegetables.

There are many ways to prepare meals that are good for you and taste great. As you become a more experienced cook, experiment with recipes and substitutions to find the methods that work best for you.

METRIC CONVERSIONS

Cooks in the United States measure both liquid and solid ingredients using standard containers based on the 8-ounce cup and the tablespoon. These measurements are based on volume, while the metric system of measurement is based on both weight (for solids) and volume (for liquids). To convert from U.S. fluid tablespoons, ounces, quarts, and so forth to metric liters is a straightforward conversion, using the chart below. However, since solids have different weights—one cup of rice does not weigh the same as one cup of grated cheese, for example—many cooks who use the metric system have kitchen scales to weigh different ingredients. The chart below will give you a good starting point for basic conversions to the metric system.

MASS (weight)

1 ounce (oz.)	=	28.0 grams (g)
8 ounces	=	227.0 grams
1 pound (lb.) or 16 ounces	=	0.45 kilograms (kg)
2.2 pounds	=	1.0 kilogram

LIQUID VOLUME

1 teaspoon (tsp.)	=	5.0 milliliters (ml)
1 tablespoon (tbsp.)	=	15.0 milliliters
1 fluid ounce (oz.)	=	30.0 milliliters
1 cup (c.)	=	240 milliliters
1 pint (pt.)	=	480 milliliters
1 quart (qt.)	=	0.95 liters (l)
1 gallon (gal.)	=	3.80 liters

LENGTH

¼ inch (in.)	=	0.6 centimeters (cm)
½ inch	=	1.25 centimeters
1 inch	=	2.5 centimeters

TEMPERATURE

212°F	=	100°C (boiling point of water)
225°F	=	110°C
250°F	=	120°C
275°F	=	135°C
300°F	=	150°C
325°F	=	160°C
350°F	=	180°C
375°F	=	190°C
400°F	=	200°C

(To convert temperature in Fahrenheit to Celsius, subtract 32 and multiply by .56)

PAN SIZES

8-inch cake pan	= 20 x 4-centimeter cake pan
9-inch cake pan	= 23 x 3.5-centimeter cake pan
11 x 7-inch baking pan	= 28 x 18-centimeter baking pan
13 x 9-inch baking pan	= 32.5 x 23-centimeter baking pan
9 x 5-inch loaf pan	= 23 x 13-centimeter loaf pan
2-quart casserole	= 2-liter casserole

A Korean Table

Koreans take their meals at small, lightweight tables that can be moved about the house wherever people want to eat. Family members kneel or sit cross-legged at these low tables. Each diner at the table will have a plate for eating the main course, a rice bowl, chopsticks, and a warm, moist towel rolled up and waiting in a little basket. Surrounding these basic items will be a number of small bowls of kimchi and side dishes plus tiny bowls of dipping sauces. A small vase with a flower or two is usually part of the table setting.

A South Korean family gathers for the evening meal.

A Korean Menu

There are very few, if any, differences between breakfast, lunch, and dinner in Korea. Rice and kimchi are eaten at every meal. A basic meal for a rural family would be rice, soup, and kimchi. A typical meal for a family in the city might consist of rice, soup, kimchi, vegetables, and broiled or simmered meat or fish. Koreans often eat fresh fruit at the end of the meal. Crisp Asian pears, tangy apples, and golden peaches from Korean orchards are favorites. Strawberries and persimmons are enjoyed in season.

For an authentic Korean meal, try to include the colors red, green, yellow, white, and black. Contrasts are important, so serve bland rice with a spicy dish, or cold salad with a hot soup. As you sample the recipes that follow, you will discover Korean dishes that you will serve again and again.

BREAKFAST

Potato soup

Fish patties

Rice

Kimchi

SHOPPING LIST:

Produce

2 large potatoes
2 medium carrots
½ c. mushrooms
4 green onions
garlic

Dairy/Egg/Meat

2 eggs
½ lb. sole, cod, haddock or
  other whitefish

Canned/Bottled/Boxed

2 10¾-oz. cans (about 3 c.)
  beef, chicken, or vegetarian
  broth
vegetable oil
kimchi
short grain white rice

Miscellaneous

black pepper
salt

DINNER

Korean dumplings

Cold cucumber soup

Spinach salad

Barbecued beef

Rice

Kimchi*

Fresh peaches

SHOPPING LIST:

Produce

small onion
¾ c. shredded cabbage
½ c. bean sprouts
6 green onions
2 medium cucumbers
1 lb. fresh spinach
3 to 6 peaches (depending
 on size)
garlic

Dairy/Egg/Meat

¼ lb. ground beef
1 egg
1½ lb. beef sirloin tip

Canned/Bottled/Boxed

vegetable oil
rice or cider vinegar
soy sauce
short-grain white rice
kimchi
sesame oil

Miscellaneous

25 wonton skins
salt
black pepper
sesame seeds
cayenne pepper (optional)
sugar

*Since kimchi must be made many
hours in advance, you can save time by
buying it by the jar.*

Korean Basics

Rice and kimchi are the two foods that the Korean kitchen is never without. In fact, kimchi is the Korean national food that is served at every meal. There are dozens of variations of this famous pickle, which range from mild to very spicy. You can make a simple kimchi from cabbage alone, or you can substitute any combination of turnips, radishes, and cucumber for all or part of the cabbage. It can be seasoned with green onions, garlic, red pepper, and ginger root. Salted fish or shrimp can also be added. Remember, the longer kimchi sits, the spicier it will be.

Autumn is the time to prepare kimchi for the winter. Each year after the kimchi is mixed, it is placed in large jars and left to ferment for weeks. Some jars hold kimchi that is very spicy, while other jars hold milder versions. It is traditional to bury jars of kimchi in the ground to maintain the correct temperature until the pickle is ready to eat.

Kimchi, a staple of Korean cooking that accompanies nearly every meal, can be prepared to taste spicy or mild. (Recipe on page 33.)

Egg Pancake/Kye Ran P'aen K'ek

This easy-to-make garnish is used to add the "something yellow" to many Korean dishes, from fried rice to meat and vegetable stir-fries. It also adds a little healthful protein.

I egg

I tsp. vegetable oil, or
vegetable oil spray

1. Break egg into a cup and beat with fork or small whisk until all one color.

2. Put oil into small skillet and heat over low-to-medium heat.

3. Pour in beaten egg and tilt the pan back and forth to make an even layer. Cook until a circle of egg (called a pancake) forms, then turn to fry second side. Pancake should stay golden. If it browns, heat is too high.

4. Remove pancake to plate. Roll up and cut into slices ¼-inch wide. Use egg pancake strips atop any dish.

Preparation time: 5 minutes
Cooking time: 7 to 10 minutes
Use as topping or garnish

Kimchi / Kimch'i

It is fun to make kimchi yourself, but if you would rather not wait the 24 to 48 hours needed for the flavor to develop, you can buy it by the jar at large supermarkets and Asian food stores. Kimchi will keep indefinitely in the refrigerator.

5 c. green or Chinese cabbage, cut into bite-sized pieces

6 tsp. salt

2 tbsp. sugar

1 tsp. to 2 tbsp. crushed red pepper flakes

¼ tsp. finely chopped ginger root

1 clove garlic, peeled and finely chopped

2 green onions, finely chopped

1. In a large colander, mix cabbage with 5 tsp. salt. Let stand for 3 hours.

2. Rinse cabbage thoroughly two or three times. Gently squeeze out excess liquid with your hands.

3. Place the drained cabbage in a large glass or ceramic bowl. Add the remaining 1 tsp. of salt and the rest of the ingredients and mix thoroughly.

4. Cover cabbage mixture tightly with plastic wrap and let stand at room temperature for 1 or 2 days.

5. Chill kimchi before serving. Store tightly covered.

Preparation time: 45 to 60 minutes
Standing time: 3 hours plus 1 to 2 days
Makes 5 cups

White Rice/Hin Pap

For centuries Koreans have served white rice at every meal, either alone or combined with such foods as barley, millet, corn, beans, or wheat. This recipe is made with the short-grain white rice that Koreans prefer, which is tender and a little sticky. This recipe makes rather dry rice which absorbs meat juices and soups nicely. For a moister rice, follow directions on package of rice.*

2 c. short-grain white rice

2⅔ c. water

1. In a deep saucepan, bring rice and water to a boil over high heat. Boil, uncovered, for 2 to 3 minutes.

2. Cover pan, reduce heat to low, and simmer rice 20 to 25 minutes, or until all water is absorbed.

3. Remove pan from heat. Keep covered and let rice steam 10 minutes.

4. Fluff with a fork and serve hot.

Preparation time: 5 minutes
Cooking time: 32 to 38 minutes
Makes 6 c.

*If you serve rice often, you may want to buy a rice cooker, which prepares beautiful fluffy rice. What's more, it turns itself off automatically.

Noodles/Kuk Su

Whether thick or thin, noodles are added to soups, stir-fries, and steamed or simmered dishes. Egg noodles, made from durum wheat, are creamy white and mild in flavor. Cellophane noodles, made from rice, look glassy and shiny when cooked. They absorb the flavor of the foods they are cooked with.

Egg Noodles/
Kye ran kuk son

2 quarts water

7-oz. pkg. or half a 16-oz. pkg. egg noodles

1. In a large saucepan, bring water to a rapid boil over high heat. Add noodles and return to a rolling boil.

2. Cook noodles uncovered, stirring often, for 5 to 7 minutes, or until just barely soft. Test a noodle to see whether it is done by biting into it. If it has enough texture to offer a little resistance to your teeth, it is just right.

3. Drain noodles in a colander. If noodles will be used in a salad or a combination dish, rinse with cold water. If noodles will be topped with a sauce, rinse with hot water.

Preparation time: 5 minutes
Cooking time: 5 to 7 minutes
Serves 4

Cellophane Noodles/
T'u myong kuk son

3.75-oz. package cellophane noodles/sai fun

water for soaking

1. Place noodles in enough water to cover them. Soak for 10 minutes, then rinse and drain. Add to meat dishes or soups.

Preparation time: 15 minutes
Serves 2

Toasted Sesame Seeds/ Kkae Sogum

The delicious, nutty flavor of sesame seeds is heightened when the seeds are lightly toasted and crushed. Toasted sesame seeds are usually made in large quantities because they are found in so many Korean recipes. If you like, you can add a pinch of salt to the sesame seeds as you crush them.

2 tbsp. sesame seeds

1. Place sesame seeds in a small frying pan. (Do not add oil.) Cook, stirring constantly, over medium heat 2 to 4 minutes, or until golden brown. (Be careful not to burn.) Remove from heat and set aside to cool.

2. Place toasted seeds into a large bowl and crush with the back of a wooden spoon.

Preparation time: 2 minutes
Cooking time: 2 to 4 minutes
Makes 2 tbsp.

Quick Dipping Sauce

¼ c. soy sauce

½ tsp. rice or cider vinegar

½ tsp. sesame seeds

1. Mixing the sauce ingredients in a small bowl.

2. Place the dipping sauce in a bowl together with the food to be dipped on a large plate and serve.

Preparation time: 3 to 5 minutes
Makes ¼ c.

Vinegar-Soy Sauce/ *Ch'o Kanjang*

Every Korean family has its own version of this sour-and-salty sauce. It is used as a dipping sauce for fried foods and dumplings and as a dressing for vegetables. It can be sprinkled lightly over any dish. Some versions are flavored with minced garlic, chopped fresh ginger, chopped chilies or red pepper and/or sesame oil. Try this light sauce first, then experiment with other flavors.

¼ c. soy sauce

3 tbsp. rice or cider vinegar

I tsp. sugar

I tsp. finely chopped green onions

I tsp. toasted sesame seeds (see recipe on page 36)

1. Combine all ingredients in a small bowl. Stir to dissolve sugar.
2. Pour leftover sauce into glass container, cover tightly, and store in the refrigerator. It will keep for up to a week.

Preparation time: 5 to 10 minutes
Makes ½ c.

Mustard Sauce

This powerful sauce is borrowed from the Chinese. It is made in small batches because it loses its strength after about an hour.

2 tbsp. dry mustard

2 tbsp. warm water or rice vinegar

1. Stir together the mustard and water, forming a paste.
2. Set sauce aside for 15 to 30 minutes so that flavor and "heat" can develop.

Preparation time: 5 minutes
(plus standing time of 15 to 30 minutes)
Makes 3 to 4 tbsp.

Salads and Soups

Korean salads, or namul, are probably very different from the salads you are used to. Namul usually feature fresh or lightly cooked vegetables such as bean sprouts, carrots, cabbage, and cucumbers. But unlike most salads, namul can be very spicy and are eaten in very small portions with rice.

Soup can be served as a main dish at any Korean meal, including breakfast. Most soup stock is made from beef, but fish or chicken is also used. There are two categories of soup: light, clear soups seasoned with soy sauce or salt, and hearty soups that are often made with soybean paste. Traditionally, clear soups are served in the morning, and the heartier soups are for lunch or dinner.

Light, delicately flavored cold cucumber soup (top, recipe on page 42) and spinach salad (bottom, recipe on page 41) complement any meal.

Bean Sprout Salad/ Sukju Namul

Bean sprouts are the white, crunchy shoots of the mung bean that are often used in Korean soups and stir-fries.

3 c. water

3 c. fresh bean sprouts*

½ tsp. soy sauce

2 tsp. vinegar

1 tsp. sesame oil

1 tsp. sugar

¼ tsp. salt

⅛ tsp. black pepper

⅛ tsp. cayenne pepper

2 green onions, finely chopped

1 tsp. toasted sesame seeds
   (see recipe on page 36)

1. In a large saucepan, bring water to a boil over high heat. Add bean sprouts, reduce heat to medium, and cook for 2 to 3 minutes, or until crisp-tender.

2. Pour bean sprouts into a colander and rinse with cold water. Drain well and place in a large bowl.

3. In a small bowl, combine remaining ingredients and stir to dissolve sugar.

4. Pour dressing over bean sprouts, toss, and serve.

Preparation time: 15 to 20 minutes
Cooking time: 2 to 3 minutes
Serves 6

*Soybean sprouts, which have a stronger taste and smell than the sprouts from the mung bean, can be used in this recipe if they are cooked a minute or two longer.

Spinach Salad / Shigumch'i Namul

Lightly cooked vegetables, such as this spinach, seasoned with popular seasonings make delicious, nutritious additions to Korean meals. After trying this recipe with spinach, you can make it again with cucumber, peeled and cut in strips, or shredded carrots or cabbage.

1 lb. fresh spinach

½ c. water

2 tsp. soy sauce

1 tbsp. sesame oil

½ tsp. finely chopped garlic

1 tbsp. toasted sesame seeds
(see recipe on page 36)

1. Wash and dry the spinach. Take off the stems and any bad leaves.

2. In a large saucepan, bring water to a boil over high heat. Add spinach, cover, and reduce heat to medium-high. Cook for 3 to 5 minutes, or until tender but still bright green. Drain in a colander.

3. When cool, gently squeeze out excess water with your hands. Cut spinach into 2-inch lengths and place in a large bowl.

4. Add remaining ingredients and mix well. Serve at room temperature.

Preparation time: 20 minutes
Cooking time: 2 to 3 minutes
Serves 4

Cold Cucumber Soup / Oi Naeng Guk

Although you can find the cucumber all over the world, it originated in southern Asia. This soup is often served in the summer because the cucumber's crisp, refreshing taste stimulates faded hot-weather appetites. Koreans sometimes add toasted seaweed.

2 medium cucumbers, peeled

1 tbsp. soy sauce

2 tbsp. rice or cider vinegar

4 tsp. salt

1 green onion, finely chopped

1 tbsp. toasted sesame seeds
  (see recipe on page 36)

4 c. cold water

dash cayenne pepper (optional)

3 or 4 ice cubes (optional)

1. Cut cucumbers in half lengthwise and scoop out seeds with a spoon. Slice into thin half rounds.

2. In a large bowl, combine cucumbers, soy sauce, vinegar, salt, green onion, and sesame seeds. Set aside to marinate for 30 minutes.

3. Add water and stir well. Refrigerate 1 to 2 hours.

4. Before serving, sprinkle with cayenne pepper and add 3 or 4 ice cubes to keep soup cold.

*Preparation time: 20 minutes
(plus standing time of 30 minutes
and chilling time of 1 to 2 hours)
Serves 4 to 6*

Potato Soup/ _Kamja Guk_

Try eating potato soup the way the Koreans do—for breakfast.

2 large potatoes

2 medium carrots

3 c. (2 10¾-oz. cans) beef, chicken, or vegetarian broth

½ c. quartered fresh mushrooms

1 green onion, chopped

⅛ tsp. black pepper

1. Peel potatoes and carrots and cut into bite-sized pieces.

2. In a large saucepan, combine broth, potatoes, and carrots. Bring to a boil over medium-high heat, and boil for 5 to 8 minutes. Reduce heat to low, cover, and cook for 8 to 10 minutes, or until vegetables are very tender.

3. Add mushrooms, green onion, and black pepper. Stir well and cook 2 minutes more.

4. Serve hot.

Preparation time: 20 minutes
Cooking time: 20 to 22 minutes
Serves 6

*Bite-sized pieces of onion and chunks of tofu are good additions to this soup. Add onion with potatoes. Tofu should be added with mushrooms._

Chicken, Fish, and Vegetarian Dishes

Chicken, fish, tofu, and eggs are the everyday protein foods of Korea, while beef, the favorite, is reserved for special occasions. Chicken, plentiful and inexpensive, is popular because it can be cooked so many ways. Since it is mild in flavor, it takes on spicy Korean flavorings well. Chicken on the bone goes into easy long-cooking dishes, and boneless, cut-up chicken goes into quick-cooking foods.

Fish and seafood are seen in all the markets in Korea. They come from the waters that surround the peninsula nation. Salted, dried shrimp and crayfish are just as common as fresh fish. These shellfish, called crustaceans, are used as seasonings in soups and sauces.

Tofu, the white curd made from soybeans, has an unusual texture, which allows it to take in seasonings, such as soy sauce, yet stay firm enough to slice. Korean cooks often extend meats by using half meat and half tofu in stir-fries and casseroles.

Eggs are used every day in the Korean kitchen. Egg pancake (see recipe on page 32) is a favorite garnish. Beaten eggs do many jobs, from helping to seal dumplings to coating fish before frying.

Glazed chicken wings (top, recipe page 48) are baked in a tangy sauce. Protein-packed fish patties (bottom, recipe page 49) make a savory entrée.

Mixed Vegetables with Noodles / *Chap Ch'ae*

This popular dish can also be prepared with thinly sliced beef, pork, or firm tofu.

4 tbsp. soy sauce

2 tsp. sugar

½ tsp. finely chopped garlic

4 tsp. toasted sesame seeds (see recipe on page 36)

4 oz. boneless, skinless chicken breast halves, cut into ¾-inch pieces

6 tbsp. vegetable oil

8 oz. fresh mushrooms, preferably shiitake, sliced

1 large onion, peeled and chopped

3 to 4 medium carrots, peeled and cut into thin 2-inch strips

1 c. fresh or canned bean sprouts

½ c. cleaned and chopped fresh spinach

5 oz. cellophane noodles

5 tsp. sesame oil

egg pancake (see recipe on page 32)

1. In a medium bowl, combine 2 tbsp. soy sauce, 1 tsp. sugar, garlic, 2 tsp. sesame seeds, and chicken. Set aside.

2. In a large frying pan or wok, heat 1 tbsp. vegetable oil over high heat for 1 minute. Add chicken and fry, stirring frequently, for 2 to 3 minutes, or until white and tender. Place chicken in large covered bowl.

3. Wash and dry pan. In the same pan, heat 1 tbsp. oil over high heat for 1 minute. Add mushrooms and cook, stirring frequently, for 1 minute, or until soft. Add to chicken. Repeat with remaining vegetables, cooking each one separately. You won't need to wash the pan between vegetables.

4. Cook and drain noodles according to recipe on page 35. Cut noodles into 3-inch lengths. Add to chicken.

5. Add 2 tbsp. soy sauce, 1 tsp. sugar, 2 tsp. sesame seeds, and 5 tsp. sesame oil to chicken mixture and mix thoroughly. Serve warm, garnished with egg pancake.

Preparation time: 30 to 40 minutes
Cooking time: 15 minutes
Serves 4

Glazed Chicken Wings/ *Tak Nalgae T'wigim*

This is just one of the many ways to prepare chicken Korean-style. For a slightly different flavor, substitute honey for the sugar and add a sprinkling of toasted sesame seeds.

12 chicken wings (about 2 lbs.)

½ c. flour

⅓ c. soy sauce

1 tsp. lemon juice

2 tsp. oyster sauce

2 tbsp. sugar

1 clove garlic, peeled and finely chopped

¼ tsp. finely chopped ginger root

vegetable oil for frying

*If you purchase chicken pieces called drumettes, you won't have to take time to cut up the wings.

1. Heat oven to 400°F. Spray a 13 x 9-inch pan with vegetable oil spray.

2. Cut each chicken wing at joints to make 3 pieces and discard tip. Cut off excess skin and discard.*

3. Put flour into a large plastic bag. Add chicken pieces, twist bag closed, and shake until chicken is completely coated with flour.

4. Place flour-coated chicken pieces in pan in a single layer. Bake uncovered for 15 minutes.

5. Combine soy sauce, lemon juice, oyster sauce, sugar, garlic, and ginger root in small pan. Bring to a boil over high heat. Remove from heat.

6. Pour soy sauce mixture evenly over wings. Bake uncovered 10 to 12 minutes longer, or until juice of chicken is no longer pink when the centers of the thickest parts are cut.

Preparation time: 20 to 25 minutes
Cooking time: 25 to 27 minutes
Makes 24 pieces

Fish Patties/ *Saeng Son Jon*

With water on three sides of Korea, fish is served often in the country. If you use frozen fish, be sure it is completely thawed before mixing it with other ingredients.

2 eggs, beaten

½ tsp. salt

⅛ tsp. black pepper

⅛ tsp. finely chopped garlic

2 tbsp. finely chopped green onions, green part only

1 c. chopped sole, cod, haddock, or any other whitefish (½ lb.)

1 tbsp. vegetable oil

1. Combine eggs, salt, black pepper, garlic, green onions, and fish in a large bowl and mix well.

2. In a wok or large frying pan, heat oil over high heat for 1 minute. Drop tablespoons of the fish mixture into oil to make 2-inch patties. Fry patties 2 minutes per side, or until firm and starting to brown.

3. Serve hot with vinegar-soy sauce (see recipe on page 37) and rice.

Preparation time: 10 minutes
Cooking time: 10 minutes
Serves 4

Soy-Sesame Tofu / To-fu Jo Rim

The mild, cream-colored bean curd called tofu takes readily to the typical Korean flavorings: garlic, green onions, sesame seeds, and soy sauce.

1 lb. firm tofu

⅛ tsp. salt

4 tbsp. soy sauce

1½ tsp. sugar

½ tsp. sesame oil

2 tsp. toasted sesame seeds (see recipe on page 36)

dash of black pepper

3 green onions, sliced

1 clove garlic, crushed or minced

1 tbsp. water

2 to 3 tsp. vegetable oil

1. Slice the tofu into ½-inch slices. Sprinkle lightly with salt. Let salted tofu stand a few minutes. Using a paper towel, pat the tofu dry.

2. Mix the soy sauce, sugar, sesame oil, sesame seeds, pepper, green onions, garlic, and water in a 1-cup measuring cup. Stir this sauce until sugar dissolves.

3. Swirl the oil in a large skillet. Heat over medium-high heat. Fry the tofu slices until golden brown, turning once.

4. One by one, dip the fried tofu slices in the sauce and return to the skillet, making layers. Pour the rest of the sauce over tofu.

5. Cook tofu and sauce over medium heat about 5 minutes, or until tofu soaks up sauce. Serve with rice, vegetables, and salad.

Preparation time: 15 minutes
Cooking time: 10 to 15 minutes
Serves 4

Beef Dishes

Though pork, chicken, and fish are served often, beef is the Korean meat of choice. Since red meat is expensive, large amounts of beef or pork are seldom served. Instead, small portions of meat are combined with lots of vegetables and traditional seasonings in combinations such as mixed vegetables with noodles (see recipe page 46).

Another thing about Koreans' use of meat is that they will use both the meat and the vegetables that look best at the market, cooking them slowly or quickly, as dictated by the day's activities. Thus barbecued beef (see recipe page 54) may be made with sliced pork or tofu rather than beef.

Some of the most popular Korean dishes are charcoal grilled, a delicious way to cook meat. You can also broil these dishes.

Koreans prefer to use very little oil in their cooking, even when frying or stir-frying. Stir-frying is a favorite way to cook vegetables because they remain crisp and colorful. Because it's such a quick method, be sure to have all your ingredients chopped and ready before you start to stir-fry.

Barbecued beef is a hearty, spicy dish (recipe on page 54). Serve with spinach salad (recipe on page 41) and white rice (recipe on page 34).

Barbecued Beef/ *Pulgogi*

Next to kimchi, pulgogi may be Korea's best-known dish. Thin strips of spicy beef are cooked over a pulgogi, a dome-shaped charcoal grill. Although it is often eaten during the summer as picnic fare, this dish is good any time. Thinly sliced pork loin or tofu can be substituted for the beef.

4 tbsp. soy sauce

2 tbsp. sesame oil

2 tbsp. sugar

½ tsp. black pepper

I clove garlic, peeled and finely chopped

4 tbsp. finely chopped green onions

I tbsp. toasted sesame seeds (see recipe on page 36)

1½ lb. beef sirloin tip

1. In a large bowl, combine soy sauce, sesame oil, sugar, black pepper, garlic, green onions, and sesame seeds.

2. Slice beef thinly into ½ x 2-inch pieces. Add meat to soy sauce mixture in bowl and mix well. Cover and refrigerate 1 to 2 hours.

3. Preheat oven to broil, or have an adult start the charcoal grill.

4. Broil on broiler rack or grill meat for 2 to 3 minutes per side, or until brown.

5. Serve with vegetable side dishes—such as zucchini or spinach—and rice.*

Preparation time: 25 to 25 minutes
(plus chilling time of 1 to 2 hours)
Cooking time: 4 to 6 minutes
Serves 6

*Barbecued beef or pork also works well as a finger food. Place several slices of beef on a leaf of romaine lettuce and top it with 2 tsp. of hot cooked rice and a dash of cayenne pepper. Roll up the leaf and enjoy.

Simmered Beef Short Ribs/ Kalbi Jjim

In Korea, simmered beef short ribs are prepared for festive occasions, particularly birthdays and New Year's celebrations. This winter dish is popular with cooks because it is so easy to make.

2½ lb. lean beef short ribs

½ c. water

½ c. soy sauce

2 tsp. sesame oil

¼ c. sugar

½ tsp. black pepper

1 clove garlic, peeled and chopped

2 onions, peeled and chopped

4 large carrots, peeled and chopped

3½ tsp. toasted sesame seeds
   (see recipe on page 36)

3 green onions, finely chopped

10 fresh mushrooms, cut in half

1. Separate beef ribs and remove visible fat. Place in a large saucepan.

2. Add water to ribs. Bring to a boil over high heat. Reduce heat to medium, cover, and cook, stirring occasionally, for 1½ hours, or until meat is tender.

   If you wish, you can prepare the ribs to this point ahead of time. Cover and chill until needed. When ready to serve, remove the fat that has come to the top and return meat to saucepan.

3. Add soy sauce, sesame oil, sugar, black pepper, garlic, onions, carrots, and 2½ tsp. of the sesame seeds to the ribs and stir well. Cover, reduce heat to low, and cook about 30 minutes, or untilvegetables are tender.

4. Add green onions and mushrooms and cook 1 to 2 minutes more.

5. Garnish with remaining sesame seeds.

Preparation time: 25 minutes
Cooking time: 2 hours
Serves 4

Korean Dumplings / Mandu

These wonderful folded dumplings are usually served at winter celebrations. Making this treat will take less time if someone can help you by frying the dumplings after you fill them.

dumpling filling
(recipe follows)

25 wonton skins (square or round, about 4 inches across)

I egg, beaten

I c. vegetable oil for frying

quick dipping sauce (see recipe on page 36)

1. Prepare filling for dumplings.

2. Place one wonton skin on flat surface. Cover remaining skins with a slightly damp kitchen towel (not terry cloth) so they won't dry out.

3. Have beaten egg and a pastry brush ready. Place one wonton skin on work surface with one corner pointed upward. Brush all four edges with beaten egg. Place about 1 tbsp. of filling just above center of skin.

4. Fold wonton skin in half over filling to form a triangle or semicircle. Press edges together to seal. Repeat with remaining skins.

5. In a large frying pan or wok, heat oil over medium heat for 2 minutes. Carefully place six dumplings into oil with tongs. Fry 3 to 4 minutes, or until golden brown. Turn and fry other side 2 to 3 minutes.

6. Keep fried dumplings warm in 200°F oven while frying rest of dumplings. Serve with quick dipping sauce.

Preparation time: 60 minutes
Cooking time: 30 to 35 minutes
Serves 7 to 10

Dumpling Filling:

¼ lb. ground beef, pork, or chicken, or ½ c. cubed firm tofu

1 tbsp. vegetable oil

½ small onion, peeled and finely chopped

¾ c. shredded cabbage

½ c. chopped bean sprouts

1 green onion, finely chopped

1½ tsp. salt

black pepper to taste

1. In a large frying pan or wok, cook meat or tofu 3 to 5 minutes. If using beef or pork, use fork to break into small chunks, and drain off fat. Set meat or tofu aside. Wash pan and dry thoroughly.

2. Heat 1 tbsp. vegetable oil over high heat for 1 minute. Add onions and stir-fry 2 to 3 minutes, or until crisp-tender.

3. Add cabbage and continue to cook, stirring frequently, for another 2 to 3 minutes, or until cabbage is crisp-tender.

4. Add bean sprouts and green onion, mix well, and cook 1 to 2 minutes more. Remove pan from heat and pour vegetable mixture into a colander to drain off excess liquid.

5. Return vegetables to pan. Add meat or tofu, salt, and black pepper and mix well.

Preparation time: 10 to 15 minutes
Cooking time: 10 to 12 minutes
Makes filling for 25 wontons

Holiday and Festival Food

Celebrating holidays and festivals is a favorite activity for Koreans, whatever their age. Besides the typical celebration foods described in the introduction to this book, family favorites would be prepared and served, too.

Foods which can be taken along for a picnic on an outing, such as seaweed rice rolls (see recipe page 66), are enjoyed often from July 15 to August 15, when families take vacations.

Companies plan workers' vacations during this time because that is when children have school holidays and when the weather in the cities is very hot. University students leave their books behind for two months in the summer, going to the beach, climbing mountains, and going to temples with their classmates.

Colorful grilled beef and vegetable skewers (recipe on pages 62–63) make a memorable dish to serve with rice.

New Year's Beef-Rice Cake Soup/ Ttok-kuk

1 lb. frozen sliced rice cake*

½ lb. lean tender beef such as
    sirloin

2 tsp. soy sauce

2 tsp. sesame seeds

1 tsp. minced garlic

½ tsp. salt

dash of black pepper

8 c. beef broth

2 green onions, sliced diagonally

1 egg, beaten

*You can buy frozen rice cakes at
  Asian grocery stores.

1. Soak rice cake slices in cold water for 1 hour while preparing beef.

2. With sharp knife, slice beef into thin strips. Combine soy sauce, sesame seeds, garlic, salt, and black pepper in a small bowl. Mix beef and soy sauce mixture together.

3. In large soup kettle, stir-fry beef until meat begins to brown.

4. Add broth to beef mixture in kettle. Bring to a boil, then lower heat. Simmer, uncovered, 45 minutes.

5. To keep your hands from sticking to the rice cakes, wash thoroughly, being careful to get under your fingernails. Using your clean hands, separate each individual rice cake from the frozen clumps; this helps rice cakes cook evenly.

6. Add rice cakes to soup along with sliced onions. Cook just until rice cakes rise to the surface of the soup, 20 to 25 minutes. Do not overcook; rice cakes should be chewy.

7. Pour beaten egg into bubbling soup; stir well. Egg will cook immediately. Serve hot.

Preparation time: 15 to 20 minutes
Cooking time: 65 to 70 minutes
Serves 6 to 8

Grilled Beef and Vegetable Skewers/ San Jok

These colorful skewers of meat and vegetables are served during festive occasions, and they are especially loved by Korean children. This recipe works best with long metal skewers. If you use bamboo skewers, slice meat ¼ inch thick. If you prefer, you can fry the skewers in a little vegetable oil instead of grilling or broiling them.

1 lb. beef sirloin tip

½ c. soy sauce

2 tbsp. sugar

¼ tsp. black pepper

½ tsp. finely chopped garlic

1 c. mushrooms

3 or 4 medium carrots

1 large green pepper*

1 medium onion

1. Slice beef thinly into ½ x 2-inch pieces.

2. In a medium bowl, combine ¼ c. soy sauce, 1 tbsp. sugar, ⅛ tsp. black pepper, and ¼ tsp. garlic. Add meat, mix well, and set aside for 15 minutes.

3. While beef marinates in the soy sauce mixture, cut mushrooms in half. Peel carrots and cut into ¼ x 2-inch pieces. Cut green pepper and onion into 2 x 2-inch pieces. Set vegetables aside.

4. In a shallow bowl, combine the remaining soy sauce, sugar, black pepper, and garlic, and set aside.

5. Preheat oven to broil, or have an adult start the charcoal grill.

6. Thread one piece of meat onto a skewer, then one piece of carrot, one piece of mushroom, one piece of green pepper, and one piece of onion. Repeat sequence until five skewers are filled.

7. Dip filled skewers into the sauce, turning to coat all sides.

8. Broil or grill the meat and vegetables 6 to 8 minutes, or until meat is brown and vegetables are tender-crisp. Turn skewers often so that all sides are cooked evenly. Serve hot from skewers.

*Preparation time: 25 minutes
(plus marinating time of 15 minutes)
Cooking time: 6 to 8 minutes
Serves 5*

*Try substituting Chinese peapods or fresh or frozen sugar snap peas for the cut-up green pepper.

Five-Grain Dish / O Guk Pap

This hearty mixture is served for Tae-bo-rum. It is usually accompanied by zucchini or other squash, and dried, white daikon radish. The finished dish has a light lavender color due to the natural purple of the black beans.

¼ c. dry black beans

¼ c. dry red beans

3 c. water

¼ c. pearl barley

¼ c. millet

1 c. short-grain white rice

¼ c. pine nuts

1. Rinse the black and red beans and place in a large saucepan. Cover with water and bring beans to boil over high heat. Boil 1 minute. Take pan off heat, cover, and let stand 1 hour.

2. Drain beans. Rinse beans, drain again, and add 3 c. water. Bring to a boil over medium heat, then cover and simmer over low heat 45 minutes.

3. Stir barley into bean mixture and cook another 10 minutes.

4. Stir millet into mixture. Cook another 20 minutes.

5. Mix in rice and cook 20 to 25 minutes, checking after 10 minutes to see whether you need to add a little more water. Cook until rice and beans are tender.

6. While grains cook, toast pine nuts in dry skillet until golden. Serve in large bowl garnished with pine nuts.

Preparation time: 10 to 15 minutes,
(plus 1 hour standing time)
Cooking time: 2 hours
Serves 6 to 8

Seaweed Rice Rolls / *Kim Bap*

These rice and vegetable rolls are the Korean version of the Japanese treat called sushi. It is fun to work out combinations of fillings using tofu and colorful vegetables. With white rice and blackish green seaweed called nori, try to use the other Korean food colors—yellow, red, and green—in the fillings of the rolls. Rice rolls are a popular picnic food in Korea, and they make a good finger food for parties and festive occasions.

4 c. warm, cooked short-grain white rice (see recipe on page 34)

6 fillings of your choice: long, narrow strips of: tofu; daikon radish; red, yellow, or green bell pepper; cucumber; cooked carrot or mushrooms; avocado; egg pancake (see recipe on page 32); stir-fried, finely chopped spinach

7 sheets nori (.6 oz. package)

rice or cider vinegar

vinegar soy sauce or mustard sauce (see recipes on page 37)

1. While rice is cooking, cut the fillings so that you have two different combinations. For example, cooked carrot, red bell pepper, and green cucumber would work well, and tofu with cooked mushrooms and green bell pepper could be another combination.

2. Place a sheet of nori on a cutting board with the long side facing you. Spread ½ c. of warm rice on the bottom one-third of the nori sheet. Sprinkle the rice with a little vinegar.

3. Place three of the fillings on the rice, forming three narrow rows across the width of the rice. Gently press the filling into the rice.

4. Starting at the edge near you, roll the nori away from you, enclosing the fillings and forming a tube. Make the nori roll tight and secure. If the end of the sheet does not stick tightly, dampen the edge with a little water, and seal well.

5. Repeat until all nori sheets have been filled and rolled. At this point rolls can be chilled for later use.

6. With a sharp knife, cut the nori roll into 1-inch pieces. Serve with vinegar soy or mustard sauce (see recipe on page 37).

Preparation time: 50 to 60 minutes
Serves 8

Zucchini Pancakes / Ho Bak Jon

This is a favorite food at the time of the Harvest Moon Festival, Ch'u-sok, but it is served whenever zucchini is available.

1 small zucchini

½ red bell pepper

2 green onions

1 tsp. vegetable oil

½ tsp. sesame oil

1 c. water

1 egg

1 c. flour

½ tsp. salt

2 tsp. vegetable oil for frying

quick dipping sauce
   (see recipe on page 36)

1. Cut zucchini and red pepper into matchsticks 1½ inches long. Slice green onions diagonally.

2. In a small skillet, heat 1 tsp. vegetable oil. Add zucchini, red pepper, and onions and stir-fry 1 minute. Sprinkle with sesame oil. Remove from heat and let cool.

3. Place the water, egg, flour, and salt in a medium bowl. Beat with wire whisk or egg beater. Batter should be fairly thin.

4. Stir cooled vegetables into batter.

5. Heat 1 tsp. vegetable oil in 8-inch skillet. Pour in half the pancake batter. Turn and tilt the pan so that the batter covers the pan evenly. Cook over medium heat 3 to 4 minutes, or until golden. Using a spatula, turn the pancake and cook another 2 to 3 minutes, until golden on the bottom.

6. Repeat with second half of batter. Cut each pancake into 8 pieces. Serve with quick dipping sauce.*

For a variation, make tiny individual pancakes by frying ⅛ cup of the batter in a small nonstick skillet. These colorful little cakes, rolled up to dip in the sauce, make a very good snack.

Preparation time: 15 minutes
Cooking time: 15 minutes
Serves 4

Index

About the Authors

Okwha Chung was born in South Korea, and she moved to Minneapolis, Minnesota, in 1974. She teaches Sunday school at Minnesota's only Korean school. Chung also enjoys playing the piano and cooking Korean favorites for her family and students.

Judy Monroe, born in Duluth, Minnesota, is a clinical researcher who enjoys Southeast Asian cooking. A graduate of the University of Minnesota, Monroe is also a busy freelance writer and editor. She has written 34 books, many of them for children, and 120 magazine articles, several for national cooking magazines. Her hobbies include reading, gardening, and teaching cooking.

Photo Acknowledgments

The photographs in this book are reproduced courtesy of: © Trip/T. Bognar, pp. 2–3; © Walter, Louiseann Pietrowicz/September 8th Stock, pp. 4 (both), 5 (right), 6, 30, 38, 51, 52, 58, 61, 64, 69; © Wolfgang Kaehler, p. 11; © Jeff Greenberg/Visuals Unlimited, p. 12; © AFP/CORBIS, p. 15; © Robert Fried Photography, p. 17; © Robert L. & Diane Wolfe, pp. 5 (left), 18, 44, 47; © Trip/Trip, p. 26.

Cover photos: © Walter, Louiseann Pietrowicz/September 8th Stock, all.

The illustrations on pages 7, 19, 27, 29, 31, 34, 39, 40, 43, 45, 48, 53, 54, 59, 60, 63, and 68 and the map on page 8 are by Tim Seeley.